# The Saint of Withdrawal

# The Saint of Withdrawal

Poems by Eric Schwerer

*CustomWords*

Amber:

Hope to see
your words in
print soon!

Eric
10/2012

Published by CustomWords
P.O. Box 541106
Cincinnati, OH 45254-1106

Typeset by WordTech Communications LLC, Cincinnati, OH

ISBN: 1933456477
LCCN: 2006936876

Poetry Editor: Kevin Walzer
Business Editor: Lori Jareo

Visit us on the web at www.custom-words.com

# Acknowledgments

Thank you to these literary journals in which my poems appeared, often under different titles and in earlier drafts.

*Artful Dodge*
*Beacon Street Review*
*Diagram*
*Elixir*
*The Journal*
*Kentucky Writing*
*The Laurel Review*
*Northwest Review*
*Paper Street*
*Poems & Plays*
*Sow's Ear Poetry Review*
*Third Coast*

*& thank you AL, your good heart and lovely ear*

# Contents

# *Withdrawal*

Then just when all the air is uniform, white,
a light rain starts

and the hill comes back.
Each blade

swollen and bright, green again
as the fog thins.

\*

What a mess this closest tree seems to want.
Its peel, black knees, grey ripples

and folds like skin. Each branch
rich with switches and twigs, and each twig

attentive with the bud
it is divining.

\*

Weird Dull Want, O Craving Matter:
what do I become by writing?

O Angry, O Mechanical Want:
what does attention merit?

\*

Now that it is almost clear
the single boulder at the crest

appears soft, tan, bent,
a grazing deer

that could look up at me
before dropping back to feeding there.

*


O Anger of Want and Disappearing: I want a *here*
where I return

to myself and not feel
with all this time I have only

overlap. O Repeated Want:
what makes anything sing?

*


And now across the hill as the air goes clear
a single boulder at the crest looks

tan and sloped like a feeding deer
but will not lift its head.

# A Dog Named Went

The room blue by day
dark by night

has a small story to tell.
A boy collects bones,

paints pictures, scotch tapes them
to his window. The mother

pulls them off.
The silly-headed sister makes pretend

cobwebs with her hair
where the glass is still sticky.

The dog lost for days.
The father thick

behind the car's windshield.
Then the four of them

at dusk in the lawn
calling *Went! Went!*

in the air. One day
the dog comes bounding back

and seasons press
like hands against glass.

## Pavilion #7

She is the cream-bodied frogs we'd find
    in the filter bins at the pool's edge
turned to dead tongues by the chlorine.

She is the reason I was the youngest
    and chosen to run down the hill to the closest
green—Meadowink—
    to scream help we need a doctor. She

is what couldn't speak, the little machine
    in me that stuttered. The woman
among the ones golfing who offered
    out her thin, freckled hand, who knew
I wasn't crying wolf. Of course

she is the woman still
    back at the top of the long hill
who'd stopped mid-twirl,
    stumbled from the pavilion,
fallen to her knees,
    was dead.

She is that part of me made to stay behind,
    who watched a man breathe into her, her belly blown
up and down beneath her skirt—the part that
    never left—each snap
popping on her Western-style shirt,
    the dull bra.

And she is all the girls behind me
    when I do get back, my mother
packing the picnic wordlessly, a tray of baked beans,
    my sister at a far table sobbing,
the freckled hand ungripping,

grass the ambulance flattens,
     empty concrete cleared for the dance,
something curling
     like a napkin
dissolving in the deep, green end.

# Self-Articulation & the Compulsion to Repeat

I asked: "Would you think it ridiculous

(expecting it to answer, like a silly child)

"To see a child who had to tell his troubles to a wall?"
Expecting it
to answer like a silly child: "Would you laugh

because no one was there to answer?"

"What is that feeling of
when no one is there?"

You see now

the crib        being held down
*stop crying*           Your parents had brought home Pistol

outside lapping at the decorative pond
*Pistol!* they were shouting

and now one of them shaking
you        saying hush

shouting *Get in here! Now!*
coming

to hold
your inconsiderable shoulders down

*What is it now?* Is it the dog
tied to your trike to get her to pull?

What is it now?

n't fully understand it

n't full
*What is it now*      pushing past you

rushing down the hall      lurching
toward the toilet bowl

He feels scratchy
smells sour

and      *You remember now?*
Here is the dimple

of a little knuckle,
the corner where

your shoe made bruises
on the floor,

a pretend friend
listening inside the wall

## How Attractive Apill Is

I rmeeber his momn had djust tdied
and he was forurious when my now mom
gently suggewsted
that maybe ther was tno need to frefil the valium
and he harked
yes ther is!

# Seaside Boy

1

I told him he should write a story
about driving to the beach

with his family. How his father
played War on the radio.

And how there they would be
Saturday morning, early,

unpacking the back of the wagon into the cottage.
I told him

people would be interested
in the pictures his mother painted—

his sister and his father and himself
walking below the slight shelf

the tide made at night and now
licked again as if

sand were the glass it could become.
If he awoke early enough

it was just the skittish sandpipers and ethnic grandfathers
fishing, his sister and his father

walking. His mother in a sweatshirt
making pictures. A kite

tugging his thin arms, the string
taut and disappearing up in the dusk.

2

I said, remember the sea's
shells? Fragments,

echoes, he said. No,
I said, remember the jelly fish?

The sting, he said,
was worse than pissing after sex.

But the boardwalk, adolescence, I persisted,
were not these at least things

the night held safely? The pinball's ring,
donuts toasting into the salt air,

a seagull's wing, sun-stroked
boards smooth as the nails' mooned heads,

bumper cars sparking against the steel ceiling,
the marquee glazing your mother's eye?


3

When it rained, he said, the sand made a crust.
The ocean became self-conscious and jealous,

stopped its affectionate lapping,
held back and grew into a bitter stew.

The palm trees fussed like tourists
and the dune grass whipped up sharp.

I was wearing a black t-shirt, he said,
that was melting into my heart.

Beneath our cottage porch
strips of sand dimpled

like drip marks eaten into rock
while the sand directly beneath the boards

stayed soft. Did you play under there
after it stopped raining, I asked,

to not complicate anything?


4

Dear Mister Misty, how much for it,
how much for all that is misty?

The nails floated out
of the shrinking boardwalk's grip. Oh

it rained every other day and *faggot*!
a smart-ass screeched.

I did not think that I was gay, he said,
but it made me suddenly flee

the noisy arcade.
                    In the Sand Shop,

he told me, there was a picture
hanging above the post-card rack. A figure

yellow and slick in a jacket
walking the rainy beach alone.

The waves white with foam.
The rain diagonal, steady.

The picture changed colors
when the soft pretzel oven opened.

He was quite far away,
his bare feet a wet flash like two wings

beating a reflection above the sand.

# Hole

There was the hole my sister pushed me in.
There was the hole she dug herself.
There was the tunnel the hole became.
There were the roots we dug around, one
rock we wore our hands against,
pushed with our heels, hauled
up into the light then let thud
like breath knocked out of accident.

Was the fact I climbed back in.
Was how the dampness had a chest.
When we hit the end
was where we found the sandstone's
thinly layered bricks.
We pulled out pieces
to make shelves in that subterranean cliff.
Thought of what we'd fill them with.

In the next day in the bad light
there was my sister, flattened match pack in her hand,
holographic picture on the flap of
spheres of outerspace, Arabia,
or other distant ornaments. There was
her thumb and sucking hiss
then soft haze filling the cave
with dull and foreign light.

She said this is what we need:
space for two-thirds of sea-
green marble; in this cubby, she said, we'll
put pappy's knife; here, the perfect place
for my little novel; yes here our dead
mother's three barrettes. There was a shelf in the layers
near our knees for three glass jars with lids
screwed tight. For air, she said, in emergency.

Later that summer she sank a pipe.
From up above, her smiling eye.
She climbed in and told the rest:
two kids had finished digging an enormous pit
at the beach. When the older one, the girl,
went in for one last scoop, all the sand collapsed.
*What then*, I asked.

In our dark place
and in our little air, my sister said they couldn't find her

for what seemed like hours. The boy screamed
for help from others on the beach. A man walked over,
said you're kidding, ain't nobody there. *He thought
it was a trick*, my sister said. They dug and dug. They dug
their fingers raw. *This isn't sand*, I said. *No, it's dirt*,
my sister said. But we huddled and we felt
the mother's gritty hands, her swollen, muffled shouts.

# What the Drowning Do

Monday something brushed the diver's chest, he reached
    but lost it to the blackness. Toward dusk
he hugged a small tire up from thirty feet,
        sat on the shore, and wept.
In time the child would do what all the drowned
    have done—surface, be found. I can't remember
why they knew that lake was where she was.
    I was 22, had read it in the local news,

in the breakfast nook, a space swallowed
    by two facing hutches my girlfriend's father
had made for each corner. It's remarkable
        the story even caught my eye
amid that drift of bills and circulars, crayons
    and margarine tubs. Maybe it was
something about an open door, cigarettes at the edge
    of the water, the word *abandoned*. My girlfriend

would have been behind her house
    avoiding us, crying in the garage, fighting
upstairs with her mom. I didn't know
        —none of us did—the family of that drowned girl.
Little Jana and I were alone at the cluttered table
    eating or not eating or coloring—learning
where clean bibs were kept and how to keep
    her hair behind her ear. I'd learned already

to gasp like the rest, to stand so fast my chair
    shuddered on the floor, to grab her
back from the glass. Or in the den to snatch her
        from the TV before it collapsed. And soon
I'd learn to kiss apologies
    against her protests, nuzzle my nose into her neck,
feel her gulp for air, inhale the live smell
    of each sweet shriek as I held on to her.

# Quintessence

Uncle Bimmy lived up Breakneck
in a doublewide that sat out back
the property of Grandpa Heck.

He'd flick his cigarette then smack
a stick against the fence and
we'd come zinging up the lot.

Kneeling in the pungent dust
the evening cast about his home
he'd drag the heavy stone off

his well—we'd gather round—creep
closer—peering down—as one
good hand stirred away the webs

knit above the dankness. He'd speak
of vapor that wasn't vapor—
of smoke that stunk like breath—like hell—

the spore of something smoldering—
a seething in the hole. He'd say
this is what we must inhale

to understand our kin. We ran
—but one—alone I put my mouth
to pipe—that rusting way back in.

# My Only Discipline

1

That clutter of apples luring drunken
bees beneath the tree? I cleared them out.
That dead patch stiffened with thatch
all summer like a killdeer's nest? I pressed
in the tines and scratched. The rake
raised blisters. The dirt
showed its dark mouth.

*He needs to learn to work! Hush, he's right out there,*
they said. They didn't know I heard.
I held my breath while I made a pass
along the footer's edge, cigarette
smoke draining through their screen.

The grass grew back in the dusk, each blade whacked,
anguished, but always coming back.
Two blighted rhododendrons crouched
against a concrete stoop, the mailbox's cardinal
boasted from his breast a rusted bloom.


2

A boy needs more than time to turn sour.
That old couple dead now for...what? twenty years?
The tree that dropped
such small-fisted fruit in the grass to rot is gone.
The wild honey bee is almost extinct. No one
smokes. No boy angrily toils with a pull cord and choke.

When I return to that subdivision
I find myself out on the street, night glowering
with the squat walk lights a new family has installed,
old ghosts dreaming in the air, their

lamps out in the second story. Through the thinning
woods the highway a wave that will not break
but rumbles, yawns. That house's breath
across the street still malignant
and meek. The Chem-Lawn rising
from luminous, creeping green.

# Whittling Lessons

I'm beating my head against the belly of the man
to whose home I once drove weekly
      to learn to whittle.
It's hard now as then, a boulder beneath his shirt, and
I want him never to have stopped
      trying. I am beating

my head against the belly of the man to whose home
I once drove to learn to whittle.
      It is as hard now
as then, but I want him to never have stopped
      trying to teach me.

I bang my head until his flesh gives in and I
am up to my neck inside him. In
      the guts I find my pocket knife.
(Why would he have swallowed it?)
I hold it to his enormous face,
      long dead, wave it

wet before his eyes and broken beard. A hive of
blood drags inside the present tense. He is
      still missing
a knuckle and all of the finger above it.
He takes my knife in that huge hand and squints.
      Says *it won't keep an edge*

but sharpens it and
we begin to carve dogs from little blocks of oak.
      He helps me with the head,
puts his tip below its nose,
cuts the mouth.
      The next lesson we carve

chopstick-sized ribs, pull poplar strips
between our thighs and blades,
	shaving them into thin ribbons
	we are to weave into heart-bottomed baskets next visit.
And then

	I don't go back.
I am too hung-over, or
	I have a test, or
	I keep those sticks and ribbons
	for years before I burn them.
And then

I don't go back. I am cold and in need
of kindling and
	I've kept those poplar ribbons and sticks.
They torch like a large nest,
	a mess cracking up inside a pot-bellied stove
	I am still beating my head against.

## My Brother

One March he went outside and found the street
littered, alive with paper and glass.
Soon he was lost in that long trail of shatter and crumple.

Dad dealt with his absence by clearing the blacktop.
*Where can broken glass go?* he asked
the tractor, the pile of paper he burned.

The fire swallowed air and let out
dry, shuffling breaths while his shovel rasped
all day in the direction his son had gone.

One couldn't say my dad was cleaning up
after him, exactly, my brother. He
never came back. My father

buried the glass in a border around the garden,
a foot-deep furrow through which no pest
would dig. It's uncomfortable

thinking about my brother's hazardous course, the swath
that threatened each neighbor's
ability to leave, ability

to ride out of here each morning
not reminded of another's awful path.

My brother was distracted by the glamour
of not the details but the glamour
that the details made. Even my father told him

he had bright gifts. Perhaps he thought of this
as he tunneled through to another garden
where he would eat or bleed to death.

## Outside the House

1

What is the paint doing on the shutters?
These mornings of heavy dew have made it pucker—

see how it curls from the weather-widened louvers
peeling into cups that hold drops of condensation?

The morning is asking questions and the first coat is getting curious.

Lichen are stitching into the cinder and first course of siding.
Even the mortar between the blocks loosens,

falls in little litters in a rut
the eaves' drops have made
because there are no gutters and the vine

thickens to the back porch balustrade.


2

My God is a carpenter
what did this?
                In front of every question
is a hint.
            The snapdragons look devilish
amid mint that all summer flourished
and now flowers as a weed flowers—

cramped, too small to be in bloom.

3

I was very young and coveted
the strips of bark as if skin itself

was saying a terrible, child-like good-bye.
It was the first summer I'd heard the word *sycamore*.

Love was a detail dissolving into secondary tissue,
a mutiny of body and fluid. I was

putting the bark to the porch
my grandma had painted,

remembering it in pieces.
The day they framed the house

with cut nails my grandfather crossed the creek
to offer his hand.

## This Summer Will Be the Bridge

Getting his name right makes a difference. (*Bill?*
*John?*) Is he coming this time, this year, *Tim Mc*_____
     from Chicago
  with the steady demeanor
and strong hands who steps from his church van every summer
    ready to work, buddy? *Tim*

  *McClatchy?* Him with thick years upon his neck,
  plugging in prongs till they stick, fixing this and
      plumbing that, tell
    him we anxiously await
his trip. How long the winter was with the kerosene
    sick at the nozzle, running

  through portable heaters to keep the pipes from
  freezing, the tape from peeling as we put mud
      to the sheetrock,
    each socket badly throbbing
from the holes we knifed for them. *Jim!* How all spring the creek
    felt sorry for the bridge with

  a gibberish of undermining current.
  We could hear in the running boards structural
      damage. See all
    the trash that's gathered beside
the concrete pilings, the county's erosion cages?
    Junior's taken of a night

  to burning scraps from our botched projects as he
  kisses that youngest Garrett near the water.
      You can help us
    fix all of this. First we'll strip
the bridge down to the steel frame, bolt on new wood, and let
    the Catholic kids you bring

  each retreat—each time you come—stain it, stain stick-
  ing to their fingers, dripping into the creek.

Junior says he'll
throw their brushes in his fire
so you all can watch the strange green burning. That girl a
flame in the night beside him.

## Simply Counting on You

This is the summer that wasn't the summer
you counted up to thirty-one slowly
    while Bunk held Merle's head under the water
    in Stinking Creek. Both of you counting up slowly
around you. The thickets and briars held a green choir
of crazy pandemonium, their greedy wasp wings
    beating above the creek bank, waxy and bright.
    The creek weed had spread a carpet out to the gravel
and was frosted down with dust. It was hot there,

that bend in the summer that wasn't the creek
    you had counted on. A grotesque maple tree
    exposed to Bunk and you half its twisted roots
where the creek bent a dog's leg and ran back to the mountain.
Merle submerged in the hive of roots, three feet
    of water, such a summer, all that muddy flow.
    The sassafras mitten leaves
sucking downstream in the thick brown cream.
A yellow residue. An orange residue.
    What do you want me to remember? I know you

    are counting on me to stop at thirty-two
and let Merle come up and breathe, to look around and see
with me and Bunk the water and summer
    and mud daubers all doing dizzy detail
    into the undercut bank.
On our thighs the chigger scars
blistered from coal seams and dog holes.
    We sent our knuckles

    into the murky creek to find Merle's neck
and haul him up and say it will do. But it won't
add up to the summer you wanted. Unreliable
    and probably untrue, Merle gasps for breath,
    shakes off the water, and says to Bunk and you,
it ain't down there, I told you.

## Slapstick Hollow

The snakes have been coming all summer.
Father tells Mary Ruth: *Where there is one
there is two.* The one is shaking the dead
end of its tail outside the house.
A thousand june bugs sing from the field.

Where there is one there is another. Mary Ruth
believes him. She eyes the revolver
in his lap, the flies around the muddy ends
of his trousers. His hand over the arm
of his chair shaking out a cigarette
in a can of beer.

A rat scuttles in the coal stove pipe. The night
moves. The day still warm on the concrete
where the snake dips and sways its head, tasting
the heat with its tongue. *It'll get in here,*
Father says. Water gullies down the creek
toward the mouth of the hollow.

The night moves like a drunk man counting,
where there is one there is two. Mary thumbs
the side of her warm Coke. They both smoke
in the yellow light, the sound down
on the television. The snake singing
through the screen door, mad with heat. *I'll shoot it,*

says Mary Ruth, *Give the gun to me.*
The night moves like a drunk man counting the hairs
on his chest. Gravel
under tires. *Mother*, whispers Mary Ruth.
When the Chevy shuts off beside the house
the snake goes quiet. *Mad with heat,*

Father says, *Crazy with it.* The question is
where is the other. A thousand june bugs
sing from the field. A cock questions

the dark with its screech. *Plunk*
of the car door. A drunk man counting,
plucking each one as he goes, placing them

in the palm of Mary Ruth. One thousand one,
one thousand two. Her hand has never held
a thing so heavy.

## Mom Blank

She thinks this summer will be hot.
Already she feels the windows stick and her back
cringes at the thought of heavy plants
swollen in the pantry. She sweeps
a storm from the porch, down each step,
then whisks the spray across the patio.
The maple's winged seeds have fallen.
One shoot spindles from between two stones
—she could bend and weed it, but it
won't root. The sky is gray, proud blue.

Already something—nothing immediate
or neat—is wrong. She might call someone
on the phone. There is a stool just inside
where the cord reaches. The thought of a friend
grows tight in her neck. She feels the nag
of her mother scolding her to feel fortunate, the wet
demands of her brother, her son's sour breath
saying *sometimes a boy just needs one breast.*

I will take anything from where you came,
the day the rain fell light and thin and you
and Pap sat and cast flour,
watched it billow
between each wet dash.
                          I'll take that
afternoon's milky pallor, the pantry's trap
that pinched your brother, the fall from the swing
that gave one eye color.
                          I will add
the slack let from the swing's chain each year
the tree got taller, the fat branch farther,
the trunk ringing from the oven ground.

# *Work*

## 1

I wake in the cold barn, scooping feed
by the pound, imagining I eat it myself,
like someone lonely and deciding to stay lonely,
treating his soul as a starving thing, slowly
becoming something else. I come back to the chore
and see that when the cows feed they eat
like me, the way all animals eat. Later I lift
my head from a plate, lift a glass
to drink, carry both to the sink, while outside
all the mouths and dull chins drop, snort
dusty grain, hull and seed. A faint grassy
smell stirs in them the memory of spring's
quicker gait when as a herd they nearly gallop
like ponies to the wet weeds along the bank.
*Ah*, I think, *that is the part that is like me*. But then
the ponies lull and graze, all summer turning
back into cows. Every evening I watch through the window
above my sink their hungry story going dark.

## 2

At the mill the man who weighs my corn
also holds the form where one selects the portions
of sweetening, oats, and vitamins that one wants added in.
It's whatever you want, he tells me when I tell him
this is my first time alone. I pause and think. *Don't
take additives, add an extra pound of sugar, that's what
Pap always did*. Done. An hour—50 bags,
2 tons. The springs almost touch the frame.
I keep it to a crawl going home. All evening
the truck's bed sighs and rises, the barn slants
with yellow light, burlap reddens
my arms as I load the bin. Beneath the floor

the bull shuffles in, noses empty boards. He
blows out a dry cough, rasps. Some things
never are enough—the metal scoop I grip,
the sweet fodder filling his trough.

## *You say you feel like a bird:*

hollow-boned. Wind
might chime if you were to fly
through it. You feel fragile
and responsible for the harm
the world could do to you, to it,
with no word for what surrounds your skeleton.

You are mistaken
for nothing perched on a limb
nodding outside a window.
A girl inside looks once and doesn't see.
Your feathers and beak
no more than singing through leaves
or bud-tips rapping the glass.

The girl inside
has accidentally snapped
the complicated sail off a boat
made of glass. Her room
a semi-gloss blue as the shell
you once broke through.
                        With one eye
you watch her look from the bedroom
toward the hall. The crow's nest
pinched in her fingers
as if she were lifting a foil scrap from trash.

Secretly then she puts it back. How
willingly it goes. The boat
afloat on its lace sea—
the rigging back in line atop the wooden vanity,
each thread taut again
with the glass blower's frozen breath and

no breeze inside to test the fracture,
no bird to report the crack.

## The Grackle

What makes the grackle not a song bird
is the way it hoards, not its cackle,
which begins with a dry chuckle, tin
foil being crumpled, then quickly winds
to a party-favor whistle and
finishes as a not un-pretty
five note song: *krrr chck, ooo-ba-leek.*

Take this one, pigeon-hopping near me—
there's two plump, white popcorn kernels
in her beak, but she won't eat. She can't
get her mind off the other twenty
I've scattered beneath the feeder.
Now a male (I think) (his purplish

sheen a bit more glossy) sucks
at the suet. Both he
and it haphazardly swing
from a little metal chain, his beak deep
in beef fat between the plastic bars
of the suet cage. This is what I mean:

the suet was meant for woodpeckers
who do not lurch but light in flashes
—salt-and-peppered, sleek, their feet
un-reptilian, unlike pigeons.
And the popcorn was meant for me,
who didn't finish it, tossed what I didn't,
hoped for a single dove (who,
when alone, is something like a spirit).

What finally makes the grackle not lyrical
are the hot eyes it pilfers from the sun.
Roosting nightly on its rim—that lip
inside of which the larva of a black hole burns—
the bird stares and stares, cocking and
re-cocking its quizzical instrument
beneath a greasy, ungodly head.

# Remedy

To be in any form, what is that?
The farmer's girl boiling cattails in a kettle

on the rise beyond the barn. Another rise, another barn
in the near distance. As notebooks full with pages

there are rises and barns, a series
of histories—families on rises with barns.

The girl moves gingerly about the kettle, both
small words on a page that is the field her father owns.

What is a nearest neighbor? What is medicine?
The wine rising up from there, the stew,

the steam and the odor. Look in the kettle
at the acrid broth roiling against the cast metal.

It's cold now and evening. Each day a thinning
framed on both sides by dusk that dampens

down the mood, eating it, forcing the steam
to thicken. When the fire began

the hay flamed into tooth straw like flux.
Now in the shoats' pen the water trough

reflects the moon—a dark flicker. Every fall
these chores become more difficult,

her fire and kettle (*boil those cattails*) increase
in tediousness. The girl's diminishing form

lacks any obvious utility
yet the remedy quickens.

The shape seen from beyond the rise beyond the barn
of the girl and the kettle in profile

bonds itself into a question, a scene
asking what wine, stew, or broth

becomes extracted by this process?
The silo's top resembles a witch's hat.

From the farmhouse a light is lighting
a rectangle on the dying grass. A thousand

*thous* and *ands* from the insects, a tangle
of bracken, panting feet

trying to beat the darkness back
toward the thorny forest. The father's bothered mind

hurrying through a scuffle of chores
in the barn—a shuffle of leather and metal—.

She stirs the stew,
the broth, the wine inside the kettle,

making only odor, warm, nocturnal, and feline.
Everything not useful is divine.

# Modern Medicine

Medicine smiles. God asks. Modern
Madacana smiles. God for more. Modern
Medecene smiles. God please. Modern

Midicini smiles. God make. Modern
Modocono smiles. God some. Modern
Muducunu smiles. God more. Modern
Mydycyny. Water.

# Swamp Girl

### 1

The water is blushing
a mirror image in the sky.

Because of the quantity of tannins
the quality is tarnished,

because therefore embarrassed by.
The swollen cypress are bathing

under the rouge moon.

### 2

Like two dozen fingers snapping
the water dripped

and pattered apart on the swamp maple leaves.
Because it had been raining

all around the water's edge
the frogs were imitating crickets

imitating dogs imitating
carpenters busy into the far reaches.

The book said *as if down the tines to the end of a comb*.
The book said *like down the teeth of a comb*.

Because the book said to the far ends of it
the dusk said *amplify, amplify*.

3

Whose light is that?
It is the neighbors'

the vicinity said to the darkness
while the marsh was listening,

while the marsh grass was glistening,
while the eyesight was wow-oh-wowing

the screened in porch.

Because therefore the neighbors
who are also on vacation.


4

So like a puzzle is poetry
which is very hard and made of wood.

Which is easy:
to like very old poetry

which is older
or to like which is like I'm so sure?

Because therefore.


5

The spring is trying to be simpler.

The Spanish moss is beards of dead colonels.
("This summa I swair I'm goin' to become mo' simpler")

Colonel Mustard is hiding amid the tupelos
chewing red blushes off the never-wets.

The lily pads've collected silver dollars from the rain
like lenses of opera glasses.

Look, there is the image of an alligator
distorting the slight current beside a rotting log

beside a white egret.
The swamp is pressed with camouflage,

aching for attention from the mossy peat,
laughing out earth-breath,

making a fog of perfume and self-esteem.
It is paranoid. It is spring.

## The New Mermaid

The air drew slowly through the screen.

The sun hung up high in the blue sky
like a hot and salty piece of meat.

The mermaid was drinking just enough to get by.

*


Sitting on the sofa her young tail awkward

as the back half of a fish as if
she were a normal little girl laboriously trying to get

a pet to conform to the lonely etiquette
of an afternoon tea party.

*


There was a sofa on the porch because the mermaid was on vacation.

When the breeze came she closed her eyes and was grateful.
*Our tails are so dry, close your eyes* an older one said *and be grateful.*

The next door neighbor's wind chimes rattled
like a crab eating the sinus in a seal's skull.

*


*It is not easy being a mermaid* her grandmother uttered *it is not easy.*
The new mermaid pouted. Salt air crammed through the tiny mesh

like microscopic shrimp that slip through a whale's baleen,
then slightly expand, apostrophes softshelling from possessiveness.

Screened inside the porch the ceiling fan spun.
From the corner of her mouth she picked a piece of sand.

She was so young
the whole world seemed dumb

and full of details.

*

On the last day of vacation she kicked her brother's ball
into the middle of the street.

This is the biological explanation for mermaids.
He ran out into it.

It was still summer.
*Promise me.*

# The Public Aquarium

The crowd looks
and presses, making union with the glass,

a disorder of skin all over the surface,
seething like a scrambled wave.

The creature will not breed
in the screened area, in the sharing tank.

A puddle slight and rank
gathers at the aquarium's base, a minor leak

between the hand rail and the ramp.
One by one the crowd uncramps.

There is a narrow opening, stunted and thought
capable of dropping a buttery thing, an amber system,

a discharge, a kind of egg.
The captive mammal does its liquid pace.

Absence leaves the echo of a mate.

# Girl Noah

## 1

It was called Noah's Ark and it didn't spin
so I went in with Gwendolyn, holding

her hand past the wooden horses, their necks
hinged, nodding from their stalls.

The floor slid beneath itself
like the top tread of an escalator

as it shook us into a narrow hall

and we had to let go. In a black room
God or Noah was cackling at the walls

and there was a constant churning
of fluorescent dust at our shoes.

The blue light lit up Gwen's teeth and blouse.
They'd put two monkeys in a jungled scene,

tails switched back and forth. A panther bayed,
its mate was not on board.
                              And then
we were outside the ark
on the opposite side of the hull.

The roller coaster swept a curve
past the tilt-a-whirl.


## 2

The dove waited in the ribs of the ark.
The Lord shut those that entered in.

There was no other listening,
just a bird, a little history.


3

What waited in the ribs of the raven?

The reptiles floated in the bilge
as if in a womb.

When the rain came
feeling was not first among the mammals, but hearing,

an incessant tapping as if from an underground tomb
—they panicked in their stalls.


4

While Noah slept he dreamt of Lamech
whose years were seven hundred

and seventy seven.
                    "The sons of God came into the daughters
of men. Their seed shall not abide

for theirs is flesh and all that is upon the earth
shall die. I am sorry I have made them."

Noah awoke and fed the ones that were dead
to the ones that were dying.


5

While Noah slept
his wife dropped a net along the bulging hull.

It sunk below the face of the water,
opened its palm,

swept through the abyss
and brought forth the uncollected, bitter fish.
                                        The dove

held her breath above the mess
Noah's wife poured upon the deck

to see if the animals would eat.


6

For seven days the dove searched across the sea.
The water swelled fifteen cubits

above the mountain of Ararat
and shimmered over the submerged grove of olive trees.


7

For seven days she was sent out again.
On the seventh month of the seventeenth day

the water receded to the mountain's peak,
the whitecaps tossed amid the leaves,

and the dove found a place to rest her feet.


8

The need to limit the number of days
is an attempt to limit the cruelty.

9

Circuses, Amusement Parks, Aquariums, and Fairs
—Come, I can take you there—I do remember

there were couples, but
often just the phosphorescent glare

of single things. A twig
limply sprouting from the grip of a concessionaire.

A hive of spun sugar hung beneath
a tin trailer's string of lights.

A pulsing behind the pressured glass,
the manta ray's rubbery shield, spine

tingling. Some magic ride ripping me
out of the grave world of gravity, whirling me

toward the thunder of big sky.

*Oh, Noah, thou must take me . . .*


10

*. . .Go away*

*now, fly little dove, I'm done with you, go. . .*


11

because I did not like to spin I went in with Gwen with in
went I spin
to like not did I because I could not ride the rides that spun I
did not I went in alone

12

Father
Sun and holy air
What is seen is made from things that do not appear


13

and the Lord said I cannot

take but one of you to come
into you to keep you alive


14

Because I did not like the rides that spun
I'd walked through Noah's Ark alone.

God I had walked through that ride often.
At Idlewild Park, at Kennywood,

ghetto of amusements, summery memory
of the oily links as I walked the plank

still sick from the stutter of the roller coaster
to put my seven tickets in the metal box.

Once inside the incandescent gloom
the plywood floor shook me through to the first room.

Two horses' hinged necks let
their dumb-eyed heads nod through the bars.

A panther rutted like a pig,
its fangs yellowed with doom.

In the narrow hall the boat rocked and I
was thrown against the rank wood—

panic in my stomach—my left hand found the dark wall
—my right fluttered against empty air—

I prayed for the floor not to move and

rushed toward the icy blue coming from the second room.
Water poured in from a loose plank.

Japheth lay fallen in an abandoned stall,
the soundtrack groaned from his plastic mouth

and in the mirrored walls
the white eyes of a girl appeared

—floating, pulsing eerily—
the flood had taken us all in queerly—

my reflected face hovered behind hers
distant and incorrectly

—there was a wind of static electricity—

what was I trying to see?—
                              Then suddenly

I was funneled out into the open air
on the other side of the ride.

The amusement park ripped up in the sun.

I stumbled down the ramp and fell
headfirst into the belly of a woman.

"I was wondering if you'd seen my daughter?"
*I went in alone.*


15

The waves come towards us.
It is midnight.

I have not bled for forty days.
Up and down the beach there are fires.

Delirious, burned, exhausted people have gathered to make them.
Ours is buried in a pocket above the slight shelf the tide has made.

Noah has banked damp sand between the flames and
            the steady northerly wind.
I stand alone, looking into the sea's vast repetition

and do not know if I wholly believe it will not rise again.

# *Pain*

Couldn't I feel some pain? Some number
of nights trying? No—
some number of nights counting one,
two, television, Harlan County

—Is it stupid saying television
watching is lonely? My hands
cut, solitary. Each finger dumb
in its skin, swollen, lonely,

overworked. Each one
— four, thumb—Television
on and on it a camera jogging
between house trailers and chain link. It turns

a corner, spot light bobbing, the criminal radiant
in the scuffle, his heavy breathing.
In two years I will marry you, something will
lift me off that couch, take me

out of that room—though there is pain
and there is counting it lets me go
down to you—Baton Rouge—
where a week before an intruder'd

pushed in the screen to your apartment.
He'd fled before you reached the stairs.
Then, an evening after months with you,
I'm storming out the back when

you scream. I look. You've followed me
and let the door slam on both your hands,
fingers stuck, unable to move,
struck hard between metal and jamb. How long

before I let you loose when there is nothing else for you
to do but twist your neck, look back
as one will do when one is forced to
lie on the ground, face down, handcuffed?

## Deep Ecology

Heidi slept in her sleeping bag on a plastic pad
on the forest floor near Prairie du Chien.

I slept on the bench above her.

We both woke up before the others
and struggled and tripped with an inflatable raft

down the bluff's steep drop
through a thicket to get to the river.

It was flooded, overcast, too hot

yet in that morning we took turns forcing
into the raft's nipple our morning breaths,

then used our hands, pushing off
against the mid-trunks of trees

to move atop the surface of the swell.
The fog steamed, the water lapped

against the limbs and

drowned brush rasped twigs against the rubber.
We floated like a crush under scrutiny,

barely touching at the knees,
her face across from me.

There are mirrors screwed against my past,
bending it, inhaling light

down a throat of artificial infinity.
A mechanical grating

was coming from downstream
the source of which we could not see.

Our hearts padding as small
turtles slid from the leaves then

dropped into the muddy whorl
churned green with close reflection.

I can still see her sleeping, the river,
the forest in sympathy.

# Central Park, Johnstown

Amid the bellowing men,
the trucks gearing off at the light,

a bird darts to a marble fountain and drinks.
Lions spout water from their mouths,

each rests a front paw on a concrete ball.
Another bird jerks, nervously preens—it is

a sequence of finches
all darting from fountain to nearby bush.

The weekend shift is removing large limbs
from the park's last sycamore.

Surprising to see the workers
in their heavy coveralls and ear protectors

remove so much with just a small saw.
Can one feel as if something always has been wrong?

In the bush there is the finches' song—a school of squeak toys—
as the branches bob and the leaves shake in clusters.

When the sections have each gone *thud*

they wheel in a mulcher.  The gasoline motor
erases the traffic, the laughter.

The birds still spark upon the wet marble.

There must be a faucet
turned off beneath the sidewalk

for at the fountain's top a cherub squeezes a carp
but no water spouts from the fish's gaping mouth.

Dry scales rub the boy.
The tail fits between his legs with an odd modesty.

A queer grin, a myth on his lips,
imperfect, imperfectly.

## It Isn't Like This

Clearly it is spring.
The bark—old scars

language has left
upon the order: a thesis of stars and frost.

Of course this is hard,
it is spring and it should be

either hard or wet. The description
should not jerk loose like winter,

a frozen slit in the frozen theater
through which rhetoric can stick a hand

to ask that we live politely shaking.
A crocus wags a loose tongue in a silly mood,

a tree grips its sticks,
blistering beneath the knuckles,

waiting for the germ like a knee
aching for humidity and heat.

A dog hit and smearing
himself off the road

toward the culvert.
The glint on the guardrail getting curious

but the metal
still curled and cold.

## Who Is The Sain To Fwithrdaywl?

What ahs loeft us here on eaerth
as it is in heaven

persisting as it never has here
is onlyt he beginning.

Who would noty be jealous?
Nothing is going to happen.

# The Saint of Withdrawal

It bats four times, soars,
changes course—scrapes black on the milkish air
joined by three more.

Ascending over the trees the other side of Monro Muffler Brake,
hurled claws,
sooty tissues tossed in the dirty white.

These are not
those birds you've seen in the moving distance
inside a daydream, slightly rising left to right,

inspiring your real eye with real flight. No. These
four have been in the dark, wet woods all night
perched in a rotten pine, standing on needles,

wings outstretched, lifted like
stooped old men in overcoats who frighten
pigeons from the park. In the weak light

two tiny dots slide on the ice of the western sky
while down on the floor these guys begin to walk,
sway and stalk, throwing forth one claw, criminal,

yoked, lurching in the quiet cold to gawk
or cock a head, moving where nothing else does
in the fog.

When Waste Management's fleet shudders
over the township blacktop, one takes flight.
It takes it

like the sick take time, taking all the air it can
each flap, coasting until it needs again, making
dashes, strikes on the sky, hooks,

burnt matches, whatever can't be taken back.

## *A Note About the Author*

Raised in Export, PA, Eric Schwerer attended Allegheny
College and The Iowa Writers' Workshop. After working as a
carpenter in Kentucky, Louisiana, and Ohio, he earned a PhD
from Ohio University. He has taught poetry to people
recovering from mental illness and now teaches in the
Creative Writing department at Johnstown's University of
Pittsburgh.  His first book, *Whittling Lessons* (a chapbook,
Finishing Line Press 2005), was nominated for an Ohioana
Book Award.

CPSIA information can be obtained at www.ICGtesting.com
Printed in the USA
BVOW022358011012

301735BV00002B/3/A

9 781933 456478